The Book of Enoch. Volume 2.

Secrets of Enoch.

Religious Literature.

CONTENT

The Book of Enoch Volume 2 (also called: Second Book of Enoch, Slavonic Enoch, and The Book of the Secrets of Enoch), is an apocalyptic text, written from a sublime view of God's heavenly order.

A book full of revelations, symbols, and great meanings, as in its beginning it says: "Enoch, a righteous man to whom the revelation of the Holy One and of Heaven was given, declared his prophecy saying: The vision of the Holy One of heaven was revealed to me… and I have understood that I will not speak for this generation but for a distant one that is to come".

The book Known as Secrets of Enoch is one of the most mysterious ancient texts to survive to the present. Almost all copies that have survived to the present are in the Old Slavonic language.

The main purpose of the Book of Secrets of Enoch is to present Enoch as the one who managed to climb to heaven to become immortal, Enoch is the one who managed to resist temptation and is rewarded by being raised to heaven above the angels. And received from God secrets that not even the angels themselves were able to know.

The text begins with the narration of Enoch, in the first person, of a journey through the ten heavens and arrives at his encounter with God. Then he narrates about the creation of the world and exposes the instructions that the Lord gave him, which he teaches his children and they must spread them on earth to all generations.

It has only been possible to preserve a text in Church Slavonic known as Enoch the Slavonic, of this apocryphal text only a few excerpts were known, which with certainty were translated from an original in the Greek language, from which it is thought that it came in turn, from a writing original Hebrew.

Regarding its date, the book is located in the first century of our era (probably from the year 70 AD). The text was lost for several centuries, then recovered and published at the end of the 19th century.

This book "Enoch 2" has been attributed to an unidentified Jewish group; others consider it to be the work of first-century Christians, and some believe it to be a later Christian work. We must emphasize that his book is not part of the Jewish or Christian canon.

Most studies on the subject consider that the Old Bulgarian version was translated from one or more lost Greek versions since the text shows some traditions that only make sense in the Greek language.

Some think that this book was known by the apostle Paul, who describes his experience when he was taken to the third heaven, 2 Corinthians 12:2-4

"I know a man in Christ, who fourteen years ago (whether in the body I do not know; whether out of the body I do not know; God knows) was caught up to the third heaven. And I know such a man (whether in the body or out of the body, I do not know; God Knows), who was caught up to paradise, where he heard ineffable words that it is given to man to express".

Some modern scholars posit that "The Book of Secrets of Enoch" was written by Rabbi Ishmael, who became a high priest after the visions of ascension to heaven.

This book is an interesting read, as it also allows us to learn many aspects about the culture and cosmic vision of the Jews of that time.

The Book of the Secrets of Enoch.

1. There existed at a certain time, a very wise man, of great virtues and abilities; and the Lord had a great appreciation and love for him.

For this reason, the Lord decided to show him the Supreme Mansions to make him an eyewitness of His Wisdom, of the inconceivable and immutable depth of the Kingdom of Almighty God, and of the most wonderful, glorious, and brilliant place where the existence of the diverse eyes of the servants of the Lord, and also of the inaccessible Throne of the Most High, and of the degrees and manifestations of the immaterial Hosts and of the ineffable ministry of the multitude of elements, as well as of the several unspeakable appearances of the song of the Cherubim Host, and of that light without limit.

2. In those days, he spoke saying: At the completion of my hundred and sixty-five years, my son Methuselah was born.

3. And after this son was born, I lived for another three hundred and sixty-five years, thus completing three hundred and sixty-five years altogether all the years of my life.

4. I was in my house, on the first day of the month, alone and resting in my bed.   I was sleeping.

5. And while I was sleeping, a great sadness came to my heart, and I was crying in my sleep with my eyes closed, and the truth is that I could not understand what was the cause of that sadness or affliction, or what would happen to me.

6. A that moment, two very tall men appeared to me, so tall that I had not seen anything like them on earth, their faces were resplendent as the Sun, and their eyes were like a flaming light, and fire came out of their mouths. Forward with dresses and songs of various kinds; his appearance was violet; with his wings more resplendent than gold itself, and his hands were whiter than the snow of the earth.

7. They were standing at the head of my bed, and suddenly they began to call me, mentioning my name.

8. Then I woke up from my dream, and I could clearly see those two men standing before me.

9. So, say hello. Their fear seized me, which the appearance of my face was transformed into one of terror, then the men spoke to me saying:

10. Do not be afraid Enoch, have courage; The Eternal Lord God has sent us for you, and behold, you will ascend to heaven with us today. Go and instruct your children and your whole family about everything they will do without you on earth and in your home, and do not allow anyone to seek you until the time when the Lord God returns you to yours.

11. So I hastened to obey his words, and went outside my house, as I was commanded, and summoned my sons Methuselah and Regim and Gaigad, and make known to them the wonders that these two men had related to me.

Chapter 2: Those Who Made Neither Heaven nor Earth

1. My children, you must listen to me: I do not know where I will go, nor what will happen to me there, that is why my children, now I will tell you nor to forget God in the face of what is vain and useless, the who did not make heaven or earth, because these will perish, as well as all those who glorify them, and may God allow their hearts to be assured in the fear of the Lord. My children, it is very important that you do not let anyone even think of

looking for me, until the time that the Lord God returns me to you.

Chapter 3: Enoch is taken to the first heaven.

1. And it came to pass after Enoch had spoke with his sons that he was taken by the angels between their wings and they carried him towards the First Heaven and he was installed in the clouds. And from there I looked, and I looked up again, and I saw the ether, and the angels left me there in the First Heaven and showed me a very large sea, much larger than the terrestrial sea.

Chapter 4: The Elders and the Ruling Angels.

1. Then the angels brought before me the elders and the rulers of the star orders, they also showed me two hundred angels, who direct the stars and do the service of the heavens, they fly with their wings and do it around each star that is looming.

Chapter 5: The treasure houses or snow deposits.

1. And from there I could took down and I saw the treasure-houses of the snow and of the Angels that guard

those great store-houses, and also the clouds from which they come, and to which they return.

Chapter 6: The treasure houses or dew deposit.

1. Also, they showed me the dew treasure houses there, as well as the olive oil deposit and its aspect and virtues; as also as all flowers of the field on earth. I also saw beyond, many angels who guarded the treasure houses of all these things, and I also saw how they are built to be open and closed.

Chapter 7: Enoch is taken to the second heaven.

1. After these things, those men took me and led me to the Second Heaven, there they showed me darkness, more impenetrable than any darkness on earth, and there I could see prisoners hanging, watching, and waiting for the great judgment without limit, and those angels were black in appearance, blacker than anything on earth, and they did not stop crying while all the hours passed.

2. Then, I spoke to the men who were next to me: "What is the reason why these are incessantly tortured?" the men answered me: "These are the apostates of God, who

did not observe the commandments of the Lord, who only took advice with their free will, and decided to separate with their prince, who is also bound in the Fifth Heaven."

3. Then, I felt great compassion for them, and they greeted me and spoke to me saying: "Man of God, pray for us to the Lord", and I answered them: "Who am I, a mortal man, who can pray for Angels? What do I know where I will go, what will happen to me, or who will be the one who will pray for me?

1. After these things, those men took me and carried me from there and led me up to the Third Heaven. And there they left me. And I could look down, and I saw the provisioning of those places, as such a thing had never been known for the highest good.

2. I saw all the sweetness of the flowering trees and could contemplate their fruits, as well as their delicious aromas, and all the delicacies that are prepared with bubbling and fragrant and perfumed exhalation.

3. Then, I could see in the center of all those trees, the tree of life, in that place, on which the Lord rests when He goes and enters paradise; and this tree is of ineffable virtue and fragrance, it also looks adorned and adorned

much more than any existing thing, and from all sides, it is seen golden and vermilion in color and like fire, moreover it covers everything, and all kinds of fruits it has engendered.

4. The root of this tree is found in the garden at the end of the earth.

5. This garden, Paradise is between corruptible and incorruptible.

6. There also there, two fountains from which flow honey and milk, and two other fountains flowed oil and wine, and they were divided into four parts and flowed around, with a quiet and restful course, and descend into the Paradise of Eden, between corruptibility and incorruptibility.

7. And from that place, they continue their course through the earth, and they returned to their circle, in the same way as other elements.

8. In this place there is no barren tree, and the whole place is blessed.

9. In this place, there are three hundred very resplendent Angels, who guard the garden and with incessant sweet singing and silent voices, serve the Lord in the passing of all hours and all days.

10. Then, I spoke saying: "How melodious is this place and how pleasant and sweet", and those men spoke to me saying:

Chapter 9: The place prepared of the righteous.

1. This place, O Enoch, has been prepared for the righteous, those who endure diversity of offenses from those who exasperate their souls, for those who turn away their eyes from all evil, and who judge justly, and give bread to the who is hungry, also cover the naked with clothes, and lift up the fallen, and help the wounded orphan and who walk impeccably before the face of the Lord, and serve only God. This place has been prepared for them as their eternal inheritance.

Chapter 10: The place prepared for the wicked.

1. Then the two men led me to the north, and showed me a terrible place there. There were all kinds of tortures, cruel darkness, and an unlit gloom. No light of any kind existed there, only a dim and constant fire, blazing upwards; and there was also a fiery river, in sight, and all that place everywhere is fire, and also everywhere is frost and ice, thirst and chill, while the bonds are very cruel, I

also saw that the Angels bear angry weapons, while imposing cruel and inhuman torture. So I said:

2. How terrible is this place! There is only pain and pain!

3. Then those men spoke to me saying: "This place, Enoch, has been prepared for those who dishonor God, and who on earth practice sin against nature, which is the corruption of children in the sodomite way.

Iniquitous who practice magic, enchantments, and satanic witchcraft, and those who boast of their evil and impious acts, who steal and lie, raise slander, also live envying, exercising resentment, fornication, murder; wicked who steal the souls of men, who see the poor and take away their goods, who being rich run over them for the merchandise of other men.

Evil ones who, having the means and the capacities to satisfy the need, make the hungry die; and having means to clothe him, they strip the poor; and those who, not Knowing their Creator, bow down before the heartless, worshiping the gods, idols, vain gods, made by their own hands, carved images that they cannot see or hear; those who practice impure deeds. This terrible place had been prepared for all of these, as an eternal inheritance.

Chapter 11: Enoch is led to the fourth heaven.

1. After these things, these men took me and left me in the Fourth Heaven. There they taught me all the successive trips and all the rays of the Sun's light. As well as the Moon.

2. So, I measured their travels and compared their light and I saw that the light of the Sun is stronger than that of the Moon.

3. I observed, that its circles and disks, are always marching like a wind that passes with a very wonderful speed, and has no rest neither in the day nor during the night.

4. I also noticed that its transit and return are accompanied by four large stars. Each star has under it, a thousand stars, to the right of the Sun´s disc, and by four to the left, each one below them contains a thousand stars, making a total of eight thousand, which rise continually with the Sun.

5. And during the day, fifteen myriads of Angels attend him, and at night, a thousand do so.

6. Also six-winged ones of them, go out with the Angels before the disk of the Sun enters the fine Flames, and it is there that a hundred angels light the Sun and make it give light.

Before we continue reading and studying the Book of Enoch's Secrets, let's consider what it tells us about Enoch, one of the first patriarchs (and prophet) of the Hebrew people.

The ideas regarding Enoch and his destiny are diverse, from believing that he became God's helper angel and counselor and patron of children who study the Torah, that God put his own crown on him and gave him seventy-two wings and numerous eyes, even believing (as Mormonism declares) that he was the one who founded the city of Zion and before the flood he was translated to heaven with all the inhabitants of the city.

For the ancient Greeks, Enoch is that character equivalent to Hermes Trismegistus, and he was the one who instructed human beings in the art of building cities and also declared several laws of great value and utility. Other ancient Jewish stories say that Enoch was a king among men, whose government or reign lasted two hundred and forty-three years, and he stood out for being a king full of wisdom and took care of teaching it to everyone who wanted to know it.

What does the Bible tell us about Enoch?

Enoch, the man who walked with God.

When we look at the current world, the advances in science, conditions very similar to Sodom and Gomorrah, and many other signs that the Lord prophesied about the end times, we have to look at our future from an eschatological perspective. The church must walk with discernment and spiritual intelligence because these are particular times.

Enoch was born and lived of God, Genesis 5:18 "Jared lived a hundred and sixty-two years, and begat Enoch"

The name Enoch means: "dedicated, consecrated, instructed". Words that let us see first the piety of his father Jared, who dedicated this son to God. Furthermore, from the Bible, we can also see that Enoch's life was a life dedicated to God.

Enoch's goal on earth was to live to do the will of the Lord. The fact that his name also means "educated" shows us that he had a teachable heart and a continuous desire to learn the things of God.

He was a person that God honored while he was on earth, brought him into his presence without living death, and honors him by mentioning him in Scripture in three different books: Genesis, Letter to the Hebrews, and the epistle of Jude. We are then before a special person and honored by God because the Lord honors those who honor him.

We can fall into the error of seeking the glory of men or the recognition of the world, but that glory is fleeting, temporary, and empty. On the other hand, the blessing that comes from God does not add sadness to it.

The Bible tells us that on a certain occasion "many of the rulers believed in Jesus, but because of the Pharisees they did not confess him, so as not to be expelled from the synagogue, because they loved the glory of men more than the glory of God" John 12:42-43.

He who lives for the glory of the world will reap retribution from the world, but he who lives for the glory of God will receive the blessing on this earth and glory in the coming kingdom.

Enoch lived on earth for 365 years.

Genesis 5:21-23 "Enoch lived sixty-five years and begat Methuselah. And Enoch walked with God, after he begot Methuselah, three hundred years, and begot sons and daughters. And all the days of Enoch were three hundred and sixty-five years."

The Bible tells us that when Enoch fathered his son Methuselah he was sixty-five years old, and after that event "Enoch walked with God." The question that arises then is what happened there that led Enoch to walk with God?

Surely Enoch had a life consecrated to God, but at the age of sixty-five, there was something that caused a greater intimacy with the Lord and a greater desire to do his will, in such a way that his life would be completely dependent on God and his purposes.

The Bible does not tell us specifically what happened at that time, what it tells us is that after begetting Methuselah Enoch walked with God. The word "beget" basically means "to put a seed into" in this case Methuselah's mother.

The name "Methuselah" has two meanings:

Javelin man. What is the javelin? It is a spear designer to be thrown. We can see here the figure of a warrior, of a soldier who goes to the battlefront with the strength and equipment to face the enemy.

Death – send. That is why "at his death, he will be sent". What would be sent when Methuselah died? What was it that was being prophesied that would be sent to earth? This tell us about the flood.

Interpreters of the Bible teach that in the same year of Methuselah's death the flood was sent. That is why he was the man who lived the longest (969 years), thus showing God his immense patience with men, waiting for them to repent.

Methuselah was then a prophetic message announcing the need for repentance before the imminent judgment that would come. Just as we are a message to the world, since we are the people who await the second coming of our Lord Jesus Christ, we announce to the world that repentance is necessary to avoid the judgment that will come on earth.

Perhaps the birth of that son caused Enoch to become more aware of his role on earth, and he then decides to walk with God as he had never done before. Enoch himself became a prophet, apparently the first on earth.

Jude 1:14-15 teaches us "Of these also Enoch, the seventh from Adam, prophesied, saying, Behold, the Lord came with tens of thousands of his holy ones, to execute judgment against all, and convict all the wicked of all the ungodly deeds that they have ungodly done, and of all the harsh things that ungodly sinners have spoken against him."

We see here the prophecy of Enoch in his time, in which he exposes the judgment that will come upon the wicked. God also used Noah before the flood announcing the need for repentance, since the Lord speaks many times and in many ways, not wanting the man to perish, but to proceed to repentance.

The Bible teaches us that Enoch was an antediluvian prophet, he was a man inspired by the Holy Spirit, and he listened to His voice because he was a friend of God. In the three hundred years that he walked with the Lord, he experienced wonderful truths and revelations from heaven.

When we decide to walk with God, our life unfolds according to the divine will, and we become instruments of channels of blessing for many people. Walking with God is not only a blessing for us but for all those around us.

We must highlight what the Bible teaches us: "Enoch walked with God." The order in which the persons "Enoch and then God" appear allows us to see the initiative and commitment of Enoch.

This man developed a friendship with the Lord, and although he lived on earth, his walk was different from the others, his steps were directed to the will of God and therefore he surely in the opposite direction for the majority of his time.

Enoch's feet did not walk the path of evil, his feet did not go to the bar or disco, and his feet were not hidden to steal or cheat. Rather, he was a man who walked in the light of God. He walked with the Lord, turning neither to the left nor to the right.

How was Enoch able to walk with God to the end?

Hebrew 11:5, 13 "By faith, Enoch was translated so as not to see death, and was not found, because God translated him. And before he was translated, he had testimony that he pleased God" – "All these died according to faith, not having received the promises, but looking at them from afar, and believing them; and greeting them, and confessing that they were stranger and pilgrims on the earth".

Before Enoch was translated, he had a testimony that pleased God. A life pleasing to God is a powerful message to heaven and on earth. Hebrews 11 teaches us about the Old Testament heroes of faith and highlights the faith of Abel, Enoch, Noah, and Abraham, among others, and verse thirteen reveals an attitude that was in the life of Enoch.

Verse thirteen teaches us that Enoch lived as a foreigner and a pilgrim on earth, that is, Enoch was aware that he was a foreigner on earth because his citizenship was heavenly, and he was a pilgrim because his destiny was to be and live with God in his kingdom. The conviction of his heavenly homeland and his eternal destiny with the Lord transformed his life so that he walked with God.

Noah was mocked when he preached among his contemporaries saying that a flood was coming since there was no rain at that time. He was considered the madman who built an ark because his God had ordered him to do so. The life of faith will always be criticized by those who do not know it.

Mockery and criticism are the weapons of the natural man that are easier to use by one who does not understand spiritual things. Jesus was criticized, Paul faced great opposition, and the early church was persecuted, but the word of God stands forever and everything the Lord has said will be so.

Verses five and six of Hebrews 11are linked: "But faith, Enoch was translated so as not to see death, and was not found, because God translated him; and before he was translated, he had testimony that he had pleased God. But without faith it is impossible to please God; for he who comes to God must believe that he is and that he is a rewarder of those who diligently seek him."

This reminds us that Enoch's faith led him to approach God believing that he was real, that he existed, and that he rewarded or rewarded those who seek him.

That is why your search for God is not in vain. For your faith, the one that leads you to seek him, the Lord will reward you, he will honor you among many, and he will reward you by giving you places of privilege, as he did which Enoch.

Be strong in God and persevere, perseverance is of great value to God, because it in itself is evidence of your faith. The lord Jesus said to the church in Philadelphia and says to us today:

"Behold, I am coming quickly; hold fast what you have, so that no one takes your crown. Whoever overcomes, I will make him a pillar in the temple of my God, and he will never leave there again. The Lord also says: "Behold, I am coming quickly, and my reward is with me, to reward each one according to his work."

God translated Enoch into heaven.

Genesis 5:24 "So Enoch walked with God, and disappeared because God took him."

This text undoubtedly teaches us something impressive, one day Enoch disappeared. One day he was no more, and I believe without a doubt that they searched for him everywhere, as Elijah's disciples did when he was caught up by God in a chariot of fire. Then they became convinced that God had taken him away.

Enoch disappeared one day, and the Bible tells us that his happened because God took him away. The expression "took him" from Genesis 5:24 is translated from the Hebrew word "lagah" which also means: taken, buy, snatch, and take someone with him.

Words that remind us that we were bought at the price of blood for God, that we will be raptured and will be forever with the Lord, and that Jesus will come as a

Bridegroom for his bride, the church, to take her to celebrate the marriage of the Lamb.

That is why Jesus said: "In my Father's house there are many mansions... I am going to prepare a place for you. And if I go and prepare a place for you, I will come again, and I will take you to myself, so that where I am, you may also be".

God transposed Enoch so that the would not see death, he would not follow the path of all. The Scripture also tells us that: "he was not found" (they looked for him, but they did not find him) that is, it was not a change of place or region, he was taken to heaven by God himself.

The biblical text says: "Because God transposed it" was a divine transfer, "transposed" is a word that is translated from the Greek term "metatídsemi" which also means: transfer, transport, and snatch, transform. That is why the

NIV says: "By faith, Enoch was taken out of this world without experiencing death; he was not found because God took him."

Something similar happened with Elijah (2 Kings 2): "Behold, a chariot of fire with horses of fire separated the two and Elijah ascended to heaven in a whirlwind" (whom they also looked for and did not find).

Just as our God raised Enoch and Elijah, Christ will return and his church will be raised. Enoch and the prophet Elijah are figure of the church that will be raised up. It is then very important to walk with God. Jesus Christ returns a second time, and as a church, we must be willing and prepared as the bride prepares for her wedding.

Sometimes we will go through trials and face obstacles that with the strength of God we will be able to overcome, and we must keep in mind the words of God that tell us: "the afflictions of the present time are not comparable with the glory to come that will be reveled in us".

Jesus Christ return a second time, we must keep our hearts prepared and walk with God. All the words of the Lord will be fulfilled and that is why the dead in Christ will certainly rise first and those of us who live will be raptured and will be with the Lord forever

We cannot forget words of the Holy Spirit through the apostle Paul:

"For the Lord he with w shout, with the voice of the archangel, and with the trumpet of God, will descend from heaven; and the dead in Christ will rise first. Then we who are alive, who are left, will be caught up together with them in the clouds to meet the Lord in the air, and so we will always be with the Lord" 1 Thessalonians 4:17-18

Given all this, we must keep our hearts prepared for the second coming of our Lord Jesus Christ.

Chapter 12: the elements that accompany the Sun.

1. Then, I looked and observed other elements of the Sun that fly, and their names are: Phoenixes and Chalkydri, wonderful and stupendous with feet and tails in the form of a lion, with the head of a crocodile. The appearance of that is purple in color, like the rainbow; and its size in nine hundred measures; and as the wings of angels are his. Each one of them has twelve wings, and they attend and accompany the Sun, generating heat and dew, as they had been ordered by the Lord.

Chapter 13: The six gates of the Sun.

1. Then, those men took me very far towards the East, and left me at the gates of the Sun, where the Sun moves forward according to the regulation of the seasons and during the year according to the circuit of the months, thus as the number of hours of the day and night as well.

2. Then, I could see the six gates of the Sun, they were open, and each gate had sixty-one stadia, and the fourth part of a stadium, so I measured them exactly, and I could

understand that their measure was that much across the which the Sun followed its path, marching towards the East, and becomes the same and rises through all the months, and then returns again from the six gates according to the course of the seasons; in this way throughout the year the sky is over after the return of the four seasons.

1. Again, those men took me to the places of the West, and showed me six great open doors, corresponding to the doors of the East. In the opposite direction, to the place where it rises, the Sun sets, according to the number of the three hundred and sixty-five days and a quarter.

2. And so again he descends to the gates of the West, drawing his lights, the greatness of his brilliance, under the earth, so that the luminosity of his crown remains in heaven with the Lord, guarded by the four hundred Angels, while the Sun goes around in a circle under the earth, and during the night it stays seven long hours; and there lies half its course under the earth, and when he

comes back approaching the East at the eighth hour of the night, he brings his lights, and his crown of radiances and the flames of the Sun waver more than the fire itself.

Chapter 15: The Guardian of the Moring Takes Form

1. At that moment, I could hear the elements of the Sun, the so-called Phoenixes and Chalkydri break into song; therefore, each bird vibrating with its wings rejoices the giver of light, and they sing their song according to the commandment of the Lord.

2. And the giver of light comes to the whole world to deliver luminosity, then it is when the guardian of the morning takes shape, this comes to be: the rays of the Sun, and the Sun of the earth that manifests and receives in resplendent light to light up the whole face of the earth; it was there when they taught me the calculations of the trips to the Sun.

3. They also showed me the doors through which the Sun enters, these are the great doors of the computation of the hours that pass each year; this is the reason why the Sun is a great creation, and its cycle lasts twenty-eight years and starts again from the beginning.

1. Those men also showed me the other route, the one followed by the Moon. I saw twelve large doors crowned from West to East where the Moon goes and returns according to the usual time.

2. Then, through the first door, it goes inwards, through the western sides of the Sun;

1) Exact thirty-one days, through the first gates. 2) Exact thirty-one days, through the second gates. 3) Thirty days exactly, through the third gate. 4) Thirty days exactly, through the fourth gate. 5) Thirty days precisely, through the fifth gate. 6) Thirty-one precise days, through the sixth gate. 7) Thirty days precisely, through the seventh gate. 8) Thirty.one precise days, through the eighth gate. 9) Thirty-one precise days, through the ninth gate. 10) Thirty days precisely, through the tenth gate. 11) Thirty-one precise days, through the eleventh gate. 12) Twenty-eight precise days, through the twelfth gate.

3. And in this way, they go through those gates of the West in the same number and order as the gates of the East follow and thus fulfill the three hundred and sixty-five and a quarter days of the solar year; while the lunar year has three hundred and fifty-four days, and there are still twelve days missing from the solar sky, which are the aspects that the Moon has throughout the year.

4. Thus, the great heaven contains five hundred and thirty-two years.

5. Thus, the fourth year of a day is omitted for three years, and the fourth years fills it in precisely.

6. Then, they are taken out of heaven for three years are not added to the number of days, because they change the compass of the years to two more new months towards the end of two more months towards the decline.

7. And at the moment when the gates of the West are closed, he returns and goes to the East to the lights, and in this way, he continues day and night around the circles of the sky, which are lower than the other circles. , and runs faster than the winds of heaven, and even more than the spirits themselves, more than the elements and angels flying; each of the angels has six wings.

8. The Moon has a six fold course in nineteen years.

Chapter 17: The magic song of the soldiers.

1. I saw soldiers who had weapons, they were in the center of heaven, they served the Lord, with eardrums and organs, with incessant voices, with a sweet voice, with a continuous, soft, loving, and varied singing, it was a

song impossible to describe, and before which each mind was alienated, I delighted listening to the song of those angels because it was wonderful and magical.

1. The men took me to the fifth heaven and left me in that place. There I could see many and countless soldiers, these are called Grigori, with human appearance, and their size was greater than that of the great giants and their withered faces, and their mouths were in perpetual silence, and there, in the fifth heaven there was service, so I told the men who were with me:

2. What is the reason that these beings are pale and gaunt, their faces melancholy, their mouths silent, and what is the reason that there is no service in heaven?

3. Then, they answered me saying: These are the Grigori, those who united with their prince Satan, rejected the Lord of Light, and after these follow those who are in immense darkness, submerged in the second heaven, and three of them came down to Earth from the Throne of the Lord to the place called Ermon, and they completely broke their vows on the shoulder of Mount Ermon.

These were they who saw the daughters of men and how good they were, and took them for wives; in this way, they perverted the earth with their actions, that in all the time of their years they lived outside all law committing vile acts, and promiscuous acts. From this situation wonderful giants were born, great men and the hostility and conflicts among themselves were very strong.

4. And for these things, the Lord God judged them with great discernment, and so they wept for their brothers, they too were punished on the great day of the Lord.

5. Then, I spoke to the Grigori saying: "I saw your brothers, and their work, and the great torments to which they were subjected, so I prayed for them, but the laws of the Lord have judged them and condemned them to live under earth until heaven and earth come to an end.

6. Then I spoke saying: "For what reason do you wait, brothers, and do not serve before the face of the Lord? And they have not placed their services before the Lord, so as not to completely violate the laws and commandments of the Lord."

7. And they listened to my warning, and therefore they spoke with the four categories of heaven, and from there while I remained with those two men, together four trumpets cried out with loud voices, and the Grigori began to sing with one voice, and their sorrowful and moving voices were raised to the presence of the Lord.

1. Then these men took me and carried me higher, to the sixth heaven. There, I could see seven congregations of angles, very bright and very glorious, and their faces resplendent more than the brightness of the Sun, shining, without any difference in their faces or in their conduct, or in their dress; and these angels create the orders and learn how the stars come out, and the changes of the Moon, in addition to good government on earth.

2. And when these angels observe perversion, they create instruction and commandments, besides loud and sweet songs, and all kinds of songs of praise.

3. I come to know, then, that these are the archangels, those who are in higher place than the angels, they measure all life in heaven and on earth, and to the angels who are in charge of the seasons and the years, to the angels that are over the rivers and over the sea, and that are over the fruits of the earth, and the angels that are over every grass, feeding everything, every living thing, and also those angels in charge of writing to all the souls of human beings, as well as all their actions, and their lives before the face of the Lord.

In the center of all these are six Phoenixes and six Cherubim, also six-winged angels, and they sing without ceasing with one voice, and that song can be described, and they rejoice before the Lord at the foot of his footstool.

Chapter 20: Enoch is raised to the seventh heaven.

1. Then, those two man raised me from the Sixth Heaven and took me to the Seventh Heaven, and there I could see a very great light and lit armies of great archangels, corporeal forces, orders and powers, and lordships, also cherubim and seraphim and beings to tremble with great terror, then those men took me and led me behind them and spoke to me saying:

2. "Do not be afraid, Enoch, have courage", and I was shown in the distance the Lord, who was sitting on a very high throne. For what can there be in the tenth heaven, if the Lord dwelt here?

3. God is the same Tenth Heaven, in the language of the Hebrews El is Called Aravath.

4. Then, I could see that all the armies of heaven descended and placed themselves on the tenth step, and according to their respective rank, they bowed down before The Lord, and again marched to their places in joy happiness, while singing their songs in the infinite light

with tender, sweet and soft voices, serving him with all honor and glory.

Chapter 21: Experiences of Enoch in the seventh, eighth and ninth heaven.

1. They stood everywhere on the throne, the cherubim and the seraphim, those with six wings and many eyes, all stood before the presence of the Lord fulfilling His command, and they covered all his throne with songs of soft voice before from the face of the Lord, saying: "Glory, Glory, Glory, Lord Governor of Hosts, all the Heavens and all the earth are full of your Glory."

2. At the moment in which I saw all those thing, those men spoke to me saying: "Enoch, in this way, up to here we have been entrusted to travel by your side"; then, those men left my side, and from that moment I could not see them anymore.

3. So, I was left alone at the end of the seventh heaven, that's why I was afraid, and I fell head-on, and I said to myself: "Sad me, what has happened to me".

4. Then, the Lord sent one of his glorious elect, the archangel Gabriel, who spoke to me saying: "Do not be

afraid, Enoch, have courage, get up before the presence of the Lord within eternity, now come with me, get up".

5. I replied to the archangel Gabriel: "My Lord, my soul has fled from my being, trembling with terror", and for that reason, I claim the men who brought me and who led me to this place, because in them I trust, and it Is with them that I can present of the Lord.

6. At that very moment, the archangel Gabriel took me and lifted me up as a leaf is carried by the wind, and left me before the presence of the Lord.

7. Then, I could see that I was in the Eighth Heaven, which is called "Muzaloth" in the Hebrew language, it is the place where the seasons change, drought, humidity, and also the change of the twelve signs if the Zodiac, which is above the seventh heaven.

8. I was also able to see the Ninth Heaven, which is called in the Hebrew language "Cuchavim", it is the place where the celestial abodes of the twelve signs of the Zodiac are.

Chapter 22: Enoch and his experiences in the tenth heaven.

1. Being in the "Aravoth", that is to say, in the Tenth Heaven, I could see the image of the Lord as red-hot iron,

it shone like fire and sparks came out of it, and they burned.

2. This was the vision that I had of the presence of the Lord, but the face of the Lord is ineffable, wonderful, and very impressive, besides being very majestic

3. Furthermore, who am I to speak of the inexplicable entity of the Lord and his marvelous and glorious face? I cannot describe the number of their many instructions, not the great diversity of their voices, nor the throne of the Lord, which is so second to none, not made by hand in its making; neither could I describe the quantity of those around his Throne, armies of Cherubim, armies of Seraphim, nor of his continuous song, nor of his immutable beauty. Who can describe the immense greatness of his Glory?

4. I was prostate, and gave honor and praise to the Lord, then the Lord spoke to me through his lips, saying:

5. "Do not fear, Enoch, have courage, get up and stand before me enter into eternity".

6. At that moment, Michael lifted me up, carrying me into the glorious and incomparable presence of the Lord.

7. Then, the Lord, putting His servants to the test, spoke to them saying: "Let Enoch stand before my Presence within Eternity", and the glorious ones, giving honor and

reverence to the Lord, responded: "Let Enoch go according to with your word".

8. Then, the Lord spoke to Michael saying: "Go and take Enoch and strip him of his earthy garments, and anoint him with my sweet and fragrant ointment, and clothe him with the clothes of my Glory."

9. At the same moment, Miguel obeyed in that way, executing the order of the Lord. He anointed me and clothed me, and the appearance of that ointment on me was more beautiful than dazzling light, and that ointment is like crystal dew, and its scent is indefinable and faint; then I looked at myself and I could see myself as one of the Glorious of the Lord.

10. Then, the Lord called another of his archangels, called "Pravuil", who has a pearl of quicker wisdom in understanding than that of the other Archangels, and it was he who wrote all the works of the Lord; and the Lord spoke to Pravuil saying: "Take out the books from my files and a quick writing reed, give it to Enoch, show him the encouraging and select books that have been written by your hand."

1. Then, the archangel Prauvil was teaching me all the works that happen in the sky, on earth, and in the sea, and those of all the elements, their comings, and goings, and the thundering of thunder, the Sun and the Moon, the ideas and changes that occur in the stars, the changes of the reasons, the years, days and hours, the running of the wind, the number of angels, and how their various songs were inspired, from All Human Things, of each human song and its life, the commandments, instructions, and of the sweet voices in its songs and of All the things that must be learned.

2. And the archangel Prauvil spoke to me saying: "All the Things that I have taught you we have written. Sit down and write about all the souls that exist in humanity. Thus, many of them have already been born; and their places are prepared for them for all eternity; because all souls have been prepared for eternity, and this has been since before the existence and formation of the world"

3. And everything is double, thirty days and thirty nights, and as it was dictated I wrote everything exactly, and in total, I wrote three hundred and sixty-six books.

Chapter 24: The work of creation

1. Then the Lord spoke to me saying: "Enoch, sit on my left side, with Gabriel.

2. There, I bowed before the Lord, and he spoke to me and said: "Enoch, beloved, all that you can see, All Things, that stand, finished I tell you even before their beginning, of what that does not exist I have created all things, and of things visible and invisible.

3. Listen to Enoch, and take my words in these expressions, because I have not even told my angels my secret, and I have not told them of their ascension, nor of my infinite dominion, in the same way, they have not understood my creative action that today I teach you.

4. Only I, since before the existence of All Visible Things, used to delve into invisible things; things like the Sun that sets from East to West, and from West to East.

5. However, even the Sun manages to achieve peace in itself, while I did not find peace in myself, because I was designing and creating All Things, and I conceived

Chapter 25: Adoil and the light

1. I arranged that from the lowest places the visible things come down from the invisible, and Adoil down very

majestic, and I watched him, and lo! That came with a belly saturated with a very great light.

2. So, I said to him: "Adoil, open yourself, and allow the visible to come out of you".

3. At that very moment, Adoil opened and a great light came out. And I was in the middle of that great light, and that is how the light of the light was born, from there a great period arose, and it showed what creations is, the same one that I was taught to create.

4. At that moment, I saw that what I had done was good.

5. So I set up for myself a throne, and di sat on it, and I said to the light: "God to the top and see for yourself on high, on the throne of the Lord, and you will be the foundation of wonderful events.

6. And above that light above on high, there is nothing else, and so I bowed and looked up from my throne.

Chapter 26: Archas is projected with force.

1. And for the second time, I ordered from the lower places saying: "Let Archas project with force." And from the invisible, Archas projected strongly, heavy, with a deep red color.

2. Then I spoke saying: "Open Archas, and let it be born from there," and he opened, and an Age appeared ahead, with great power, and also very dark, gestating the creation of All Things of down. So, I saw that thus work was good and I spoke to him saying:

3. "Go much lower and you will become firm, and be a pedestal for low things", and so it was, and he went below and fixed himself, and it was the beginning of common things, and lower than darkness there is nothing else.

Chapter 27: The first day.

1. at that time I ordered that it be taken from the light, as well as from the darkness, and I spoke saying: Become solid and so it was, and I scattered it with the light, and it became the water and scattered it on the darkness below of light, it was there when I made the water firm, that is, the bottomless one, I also made a foundation of light around the water and established seven circles inside it, and imagine the water as wet glass and dry, that is, as glass, and the circumcision of the waters and of the other elements, there I established for each one its path, and the seven stars each one of them in its sky, and that they were in the way that I established, then I saw that what was created was very good.

2. Then, between the light and the darkness, I placed a separation, that is, in the entire center of the water, here and there, I also spoke to the light saying that it should be the day, and to the darkness, that it would be the night, then the afternoon arose right there and also the dawn of the first day.

Chapter 28: Then earth and the abyss

1. At that time, I firmly established the heavenly circle, and at the same time made the waters below the sky merge with each other, in a single deep space, so that the chaos became dry, and so it has been made.

2. And in the midst of that great quantity of waves, I made the great and hard rock, and from that rock, I heaped up the dry part, and then I called the dry part earth, and the center of the earth I called the abyss, which means bottomless, and I collected the sea in one place, and with a single yoke, I bound it.

3. At that moment I spoke to the sea saying: "Observe, today I set an eternal limit for you, and you will not break your components by untying it from its parts".

4. And in this way, I quickly made the firmament. This day I called: El First Created.

I imagined the image and essence of fire, among all the celestial army, and my eye looked at the very hard and firm rock, and from the brilliance of my eye, the lightning received its natural prodigy, since both are water in fie and fire into water, and neither can be separated from the other, and neither can dry the other, therefore they ray is brighter than the Sun, softer and smoother than water and firmer than rock hard.

2. And from that rock I completely cut out a very great fire, and from the fire, I made the orders of the ten incorporeal hosts of angels, and their weapons are fiery, and their garments are like fiery flames, and by my order, each one of they were to stand in due order. Here Satan was cast down from on high with his angels.

3. And precisely, it was one of all the angelic orders who, having parted with the order that was under his authority, conceived an impossible idea: To establish his throne higher than the clouds above the earth so that he could become equal in rank to my great power.

4. Then I cast him down from above with his angels and he was continuously flying in the air, over the face of the abyss.

1. When the third day arrive, I commanded the earth to be filled with fruitful and large trees, as well as hills and seeds to sow, so I planted Paradise, I also fenced it, and I placed their angels as flaming armed guardians, and in this way I did renewal.

2. And so the night came, and the fourth day dawned again.

3. And I ordained, on the fourth day, that great lights should come into being in the heavenly circles.

4. So that in the highest and first of the circles I put the stars, Kruno, and in the second circle then Aphrodite, in the third Aris, in the fifth Zeus, in the sixth Ermis, in the seventh smaller circle I put the Moon and decorated it with the smaller stars.

5. And in the lower circle, I put the Sun so that it will light the day, and I put the Moon so that it will light the night.

6. I placed the Sun, so that it should go with each animal (relating to the signs of the Zodiac,) which are twelve, and I assigned them the course of the months, with their names and lives, their notoriety, their respective appointed hours, and the manner in which one after another should succeed one another.

7. Thus night came, and also became the morning of the fifth day.

8. I ordained on the fifth day (Thursday), that the sea should bring fish, and also feathered birds of multiple varieties, and also all kinds of animals that creep on the land, and those that move on the face of the earth. Earth on all fours, and those that rise in the air, male and female, and also every soul and living being that breathes the spirit of life.

9. And so, night came, and back came the morning of the sixth day (Friday)

10. On this sixth day, I ordered my wisdom to create the human being from seven consistencies, which are composed of:

-His meat from the land itself,

- His blood of dew,

- His eyes from the sunlight,

- From the stone come to their bones,

-His intelligence of the speed of angles and clouds,

-His hair and his veins come from the grass on the face of the earth,

- His soul of the wind and my breath.

11. I also granted seven natures to the flesh, hearing, eyes to see, soul, smell veins, touch, blood for taste, bones for strength, and intelligence speed, for you to enjoy.

12. And I conceived a subtle saying that says: I made man from the invisible and the visible nature, from both arises his death and life and image, he knows language as a created thing; to be small in greatness and again to be great in smallness. And I placed him on the face of the earth as a second angel, honorable, great and glorious, and I established him as the rulers to administer on earth and have my wisdom, and thus there was none on earth greater than him among all my existing creatures.

13. And I gave him a name of the four component parts, from the east, from the west, from the south, and decreed for him four special stars, and the name by which I called his was Adam, and I taught him the two ways, the of Light and that of darkness. And I spoke to him saying:

14. That is bad, this is good, and in this way, I would prove if he really had a love for me or perhaps hatred, and thus make It clear who among his race loved me.

15. It was clear to me how his nature was, I had already seen it, but he had not yet seen his, in this way, since he could not see through himself I knew that he would sin from bad to worse. It was there that I said to myself: "After sinning, what is left but death?"

16. So, I decided to put him to sleep, and sure enough he fell asleep. So I took a rib from him and made a wife for him so that death will come to him by his own wife. And I took her last word and gave her a name, mother, a word that means Eva.

Chapter 31: The Garden of Eden, and ignorance

1. Adam was beginning his life on earth, and I decided to create a garden in Eden in the East so that he should know and observe the testament and keep the commandment.

2. And for Adam, I caused the heavens to open, so that he could see the angels sing the hymn of victory, and the light dimmed.

3. Adam was always in Paradise; the devil understood that I planned to create another world, because Adam was the lord on earth, so he could govern and administer it.

4. The demon, the devil is that evil spirit of the nether places, and as a fugitive angel of light, he created Stone from the heavens, in the manner and manner that his name was Satan, and thus he became different from the other angels, but his nature did not change his intelligence beyond his understanding for what is right and what is sinful and immoral.

5. And the devil understood his condemnation, as well as the sin that he himself had previously committed, and therefore, he conceived a plan against Adam, in such a way that he entered Paradise, and managed to seduce Eve, but he did not touch Adam.

6. And so I cursed ignorance; but what I previously blessed, that, I do not curse. Therefore, I do not curse man, nor the earth, nor even other creatures, but, as for man, I do curse his evil fruit and the works of his hands.

Chapter 32: The seventh day and the Second Coming.

1. Then I spoke saying: "Earth you are, and to the land from which you have been taken, you must return, I will not bring3 ruin upon you, but I am sending you back to the place from which I took you."

2. In this way, I can again receive you at my second coming.

3. Behold now I bless all my creatures, the invisible and the visible. And Adam spent five and a half hours in beautiful Paradise.

4. Then I blessed the seventh day, which in the Sabbath, the day on which he rested from all the works he had done.

Chapter 33: The Eighth Day and the Books of Enoch.

1. I declared the eighth day, and this eighth day would be at the same time the first created after my work, and the first seven days would rotate in the form of the seven thousand years, and that at the beginning of the eight thousand years the time that is counted no more, days without years or month, nor weeks, nor days, no hours, nor minutes.

2. listen to me now Enoch, all the things that I have narrated to you, all that you have understood, and all that you have been able to see of heavenly things, as well as all that you have seen on earth and all that I have written in these books, due to my exalted and great wisdom, I imagined and created all things from the highest creation

to the lowest and to the end, and there is no adviser or one who inherits my creations.

3. Therefore: "I am my own Eternal, without replacement or possibility of being changed, not created by any hand.

4.From my mind comes my advice, she is my adviser, my great wisdom and my powerful word are made, and any eyes can see all things, as they are placed here and tremble with great fear.

5. All these things would come to be destroyed if I turned my face away from them.

6. Enoch, organize your mind and know the one who is speaking to you, and now take the books that you yourself have written.

7. And now I put Samuel and Raguil, they will take you with your books, and go down to earth and speak to your children and tell them all the things that I have told you, as well as all the things that you have seen from the lowest heaven to my glorious throne, with all its vast armies.

8. Well, all things and all forces were created by me, and there is nothing that resists me and is not subject to my government and my orders, all forces and all things work for me only to command.

9. Then Enoch, give your children the books of scripture in their hands, and they will read them and know me as the creator of All Things, and they will understand how it is that there is no other God, but "I"

10. And see that they make known and distribute the books that you have written with your hand, children to children, from generation to generation, from people to people, and from nation to nation.

11. And Enoch, to you I will give, my intercessor, the archangel Michael, for the writings of your father, Adam, Seth, Enos, Cainan, Mahalaleel, and Jared, your father.

Chapter 34: The rejection of the law and the Flood.

1. Sadly, they have despised my law and my commandments, they have cultivated and also gathered unworthy seeds without fearing God, and they have not loved me, because they have begun to prostate themselves before vain gods, and have denied My Unity, and have filed the earth with lies, deceit, abominable offenses, licentiousness, they have joined one another, and have practiced all kinds of immoral excesses that even generate disgust to relate.

2. And as a result of these actions, I will send a flood over the earth, and I will destroy all men, and all the earth together will be plunged into very great darkness

Chapter 35: The generation that will deliver the Book and the other that must read it.

1. The Lord concluded that from the seed of these a new generation should arise long after them, but many of these would be insatiable.

2. The one who raises that generation has the responsibility to teach and reveal these books written through your hand, as well as that of your parents, it is to them that he must point out the custody of the world, to faithful men and workers of my truth and my joy, so that my mighty name may not be unknown.

3. They must deliver this knowledge to another generation, and that to others, and having read they may be glorified forever, much more than at the time of the beginning.

Chapter 36: Books must be read and understood.

1. Enoch, listen to me because now I will give you time for thirty days so that you can be with your loved ones, in your house, and tell your children and the whole family what everyone must listen to with great attention about my Presence, what is said to them through your lips, what they must read and understand, the reason why there is no other God, but "I".

2. My laws and commandments, which they must always keep, and must begin to read and take within themselves the books written through your hand.

3. And when the thirty days are completed, I will send my angel for you, and he will be the one who took you from the earth and from among your people and brings you to my Presence.

Chapter 37: The fearsome and frosty Angel.

1. Then, at that time, God gave order that one of his oldest angels, who is challenging and fearsome, put him by my side, white as snow was his appearance, and his hands were life ice, he had the appearance of a great frosty; and so it froze my face, because I could not withstand the power of the fire kindled by the Lord, just

as it is not possible to withstand a burning stove, not the burning fire of the Sun, nor the cold frost of the air.

2. Then, I heard the voice of the Lord that spoke to me saying: "Enoch, if your face had not been frozen in this way, no human being would be able to look at your face."

Chapter 38: Enoch's return home.

1. At that time, the Lord spoke to those first men who took me up, saying: "Let Enoch come down to earth with you, and wait until the day that I have determined."

2. And that same night the men left me on my bed. And Methuselah who waited for my return kept watch day and night on my bed was filled with fear when he heard my arrival, and I spoke to him saying: "Have all my family come and meet us, in this way I will tell them everything. What happened".

Chapter 39: The prophecy of what was, what is and will be until the time of judgment.

1. As my whole family gathered, I spoke to them saying: O children, my beloved, listen carefully to your father's

warning, all the more so as it is agreed by the commandment of the Lord.

2. I was allowed to come to you today, and I announce to you, not by my own mouth, but from the mouth of the Lord, all that is and was all that is now, and all that will happen until time and Day of Judgment.

3. Well, the Lord has allowed me to come to you, that is why can listen to the words that come from my mouth, from a man-made powerful for you, because without a doubt, I am a privileged man, an anointed one who has seen the face of the Lord, like iron made to sparkle with the fire that releases flames and very strong sparks that burn.

4. You can see the prudence in my eyes because they are the eyes of a noble heart with design and meaning for your life because I have seen the eyes of the Lord, which shine like the rays of the Sun, and fill the man's eyes of a fear that glows with fire.

5. My beloved children, observe the right hand of the man who helps you; because I have seen the right hand of the Lord, which fills the sky as he helped me.

6. Now you can look at the beat of my was of working as if it were yours, but I have seen the limitless and perfect beat of the Lord, which has no end.

7. You can listen to the words that come out of mouth, just as I listen to the voice of the Lord, which is like a mighty permanent thunder among a tumult of clouds in the sky.

8. Listen, now my children, to the conversations of your father on this earth, how terrible and fearful it is to come before the ruler of the earth, how much more fearful it is to appear face to face before the Lord Almighty, the one who dominates Heaven!, who controls the swiftness and death and of the armies in the skies! Who will be the one who can resist that great endless pain?

Chapter 40: I diligently researched and wrote about All Things.

1. Now, I know All Things, because these have come from the mouth of the Lord, my children, these I could see with my eyes, from the beginning to the end.

2. I have written All Things in books, for now, I know them all, their cycles and their end, and their plenitudes, and about all hosts, as well as all their marches and order.

3. Take the measurements and make drawings of the stars, the immense and great multitude of them.

4. There is no human being who has seen their revolutions and entrances, not even the angels know their number, but I have managed to write each of their names.

5. I also took the measurements of the Sun, as well as its circumference and its powerful rays, I took account of its hours, I wrote of All Things that are on the earth, I have written about the things that are nutritious in the earth, about of all the various seeds that are planted and those that are not, and of those that the earth produces and of all the plants and every grass and every flower, as well as their respective names and their sweet fragrances, and of the places where the clouds dwell, about their compositions, and their wings, and the way the generate rain and raindrops.

6. I was also diligent in researching All Things, so I wrote about the way of thunder and also of lightning, and I was shown the keys and their guardians, their ascensions, and the way they travel; they let themselves go gently by measure by a chain, and thus supported by a strong chain and violence, el throws down the furious clouds, and All Things on earth are destroyed.

7. I was also able to write about the treasure-houses of the snow, and the storage abodes of cold and frosty airs, and I also saw the one who keeps the keys of the seasons, the one who fills the clouds with them and it does not weaken the treasure deposits.

8. I also wrote about the resting abodes of the winds, and I could observe and saw how their key-keepers supported weight scales and various measures; First they put it on one weight scale, then on the other and the weights were let out according to the measure, with skill on the face of the earth, with the purpose that by strong breathing they disposed to oscillate the earth.

9. Then I took measurements of the whole earth, its mountains and hills, as well as its fields, trees, stones, and rivers; All the Things that exist I wrote in the books, from the top of the earth to the seventh heaven and down to the very lowest hell, and the place of judgment, and the very great painful place of purification.

Chapter 41: Pain for the condition of Adam and Eve.

1. And I also saw, the ancestors of all time with Adam and Eve; at that moment I sighed sadly, and burst into tears and told myself of the ruin of his dishonor.

2. Shame is made on me for my weakness, and for that of my ancestors, and I reflected within my heart, and said:

3. Blessed is that man who has not experienced birth, and who has not sinned before the presence of the Lord, who

does not come to this place, nor bear the yoke of this place.

1. At that moment I cloud see the key-keepers, and the guards of the place of grief and tears standing up, they were similar to large snakes, and their faces were like extinguished lamps, and their eyes of intense fire, their teeth were sharp; and I could see that all the works of the Lord are just and correct, while the works of the human being are some good and others bad, and in their works, it is known about those who lie in a vile and shameful way.

1. Then there, my children, I took measures and was able to write every deed and every measure, as well as every correct act of justice.

2. And likewise, as one year is clearer than the next, so also is a man more enlightened than another, some of them because they have great possessions, others

because of their great wisdom in their hearts; those for their particular intellect, and others for their cunning; others for the silence that his mouth keeps, another also, for his purification; others for his great strength, and other for his kindness; one for his youth and others for his sharp wit; others for the beauty of her body, and others for her sensitive heart; let it be heard everywhere, but in truth be pronounced, there is nothing better than that person who respects, loves and gives glory to the Lord, he will be honored in time to come.

Chapter 44: The Contempt of the Little Ones.

1. Having created man in the image of his likeness, the Lord also made him small and great in spirit, body, and mind, in the same way in his works.

2. With a clear warning in mind, anyone who insults the face of the Lord Almighty and belittles the image of the Lord, and whoever vents his wrath on any man, God will separate him for a time and in his great love and mercy will teach him the path that he will have to find for himself, and he who in reproach spits in man's face, will find the truth in due time, and at the indicated time of judgment he will be taught the path of justice.

3. Blessed and blessed is the human being who does not carry his heart with evil and malice, who does not turn against any man, and helps the wounded, lifts the fallen, and does charity to those who are in need because in time of the great judgment each weight, each measure and each addition will be as in the market; As it were, they are weighed in scales and standing in the marketplace, and each one will know his measure, and his just reward will be according to his measure.

Chapter 45: Don't rush, act right.

1. Contrite and clean hearts, whoever, with a voluntary and diligent heart, hastens to make offerings before the presence of the Lord, for his part the Lord will make that offering faster and more blessed by offering his help.

2. But, whoever wishes to accelerate the light of his lamp before the presence of the Lord, without doing it with true judgment and with understanding, the Lord will not increase or multiply his treasure in the Kingdom on High.

3. it must be considered that when the Lord is presented with bread of candles, rams or other kinds of sacrifices, this means nothing; because in reality what God asks for

are clean and pure hearts, and with only this, the Lord tests the human heart.

Chapter 46: The deception of the "good" will be discovered.

1. My people, listen carefully and keep in your heart these words that I declare today with my mouth.

2. If any person presents gifts of gift to a ruler on earth and think in his mind with disloyalty in his heart, and the ruler knowing it is not displeased and does not return those gifts and does not deliver him to judgment? Also consider, if a person appears to be good for another, with the falsehood of his tongue, bringing deceit in his heart, would he not understand that betrayal of his heart and he will not be condemned, when that falsehood was evident in the sight of all?

3. And it will come to pass that at the time that the Lord sends forth his mighty light, then there will be judgment for the just and the unjust, and at that time no one will be able to escape being seen.

1. My children, now you must guard and settle your thought in each one of your hearts, you must seal very well the words of your father because they all come to you from the mouth of the Lord.

2. Now, take these books of scripture from my hand and you must read them.

3. Because these books are many, and in these, you are going to learn about all the works of the Lord, everything that has been since the beginning of creation, and what will be until the end times.

4. And if you read my scriptures carefully, you will not sin against the Lord; because there Is no other, except the Lord, neither in heaven, nor on earth, nor in the lowest or deepest places, there is not even one at the beginning of all things, only the Lord.

5. The Almighty Lord is the one who has started the unknown and has scattered visible and invisible skies. He was also the one who settled the earth on the waters and who created countless creatures and calculated the water and he principle of the soluble or the dust of the earth, as well as of the sand of the sea, the drops of rain, the dew

in the morning; and the breath of the wind. He is the one who filled the earth, the sea, and the unshakable winter.

6. The Lord is the one who counted the stars of the fire and decorated the sky and put in the center of everything.

Chapter 48: Read and practice the scriptures to yourself.

1. Through the seven circles, of the passage of the Sun, which come to be the convention of the one hundred and eighty-two thrones, which he makes in a short day, and again another one hundred and eighty-two, which he descends in a long day, and he has two thrones on which he rests, rotating to and fro, on the thrones of the months, from the seventeenth day of the month Tsivan, he descends to the month Thevan, and from the seventeenth of Thevan, he ascends again

2. And it is in this way that he approaches the earth, it is then that the earth rejoices and makes its fruits grow, and when he withdraws, the earth becomes sad and the trees and their fruits do not bloom.

3. In his immense wisdom, he measured all this with a good measure of all his hours, he established a measure of everything visible and invisible

4. Of all that is invisible, he made All Things visible, being in his very nature invisible.

5. in this way, my children, I make these things known to you, distribute the books to your descendants, within your generation and also among the nations that will have the sense of love for God, allow them to receive them and it may happen May they come to love them more than any sweet delicacy on earth, and may read them and put them to work among themselves.

6. And those people who understand the Lord, those who do not love God, who do not accept him, who reject and do not receive these books, an immense judgment awaits them.

7. Blessed and blessed is the human being who will carry his yokes and drag them with him because he will find freedom on the day of final judgment.

Chapter 49: The security and firmness of the Word.

1. My children, I swear to each one of you; I swear, not by any oath, nor by Heaven, nor by the earth, nor by any creature that God has created, I swear.

2. The Lord spoke saying: "There is no oath in me, neither injustice, only truth".

3. if there is no truth in the human being, let them swear by the words: Yes, yes, and also no, no".

4. And I swear to you, my children, yes, yes that there has not been any man in the womb of your mother, who has not already prepared for each one of them a place for the repose of their soul, and a certain measure how much is established for a man to be tested on this earth.

5. Yes, my children, do not deceive yourselves, because a place has previously been prepared for each one of the souls of men.

Chapter 50: Act with Justice towards the needy and Patience.

1. I have written about every one of the works of man, and there is no man born on earth who can remain hidden, nor can his works remain silent.

2. I can see all things, without exception.

3. That is why, now, my children, in a humble heart and with patience let the number of your days pass, so that you may be allowed to inherit infinite life.

4. For all this and the sake of the Lord, you must tolerate every injury, every grievance, every offense, every evil word, and every moment of aggression.

5. Do not return the evil that they have done to you, neither to a neighbor nor to any enemy, because the Lord is the one who is in charge of returning it for you, and it will be the law on the day of the great judgment because here, there should be no revenge between humans.

6. Anyone of you who does a favor with your silver or with your gold for the good of your brothers, will receive great treasure in the world to come.

7. Also, you must not revile or offend widows, orphans, or foreigners, so that the laws of God's wrath do not come upon your lives.

Chapter 51: Justice and help the poor.

1. It is very important, my children, that you extend your hand to the needy, according to your capacity.

2. Avoid hiding your money in the same land.

Bear in mind to help the faithful man in his affliction, and in this way, the affliction will not find you in the time of your need.

4. And every yoke of affliction and cruelty that comes upon you, bear it because of the name of the Lord, then you will find your reward in the time of judgment.

5. Remember that it is very good to go in the morning, at noon, in the afternoon, and at night to the abode of the Lord for the honor and glory of your Creator.

6. Because everything that breathes glorifies him, and every invisible and visible creature, in this way returns praise to him.

Chapter 52: Justice and injustices will be weighed.

1. Happy and blessed is the man who opens his mouth in honor and praise to the God of the Sabbath and exalts the Lord in his heart.

2. Abominable and depraved is the man who opens his mouth to insult and slander his neighbor because he attracts the contempt of the Lord upon his life.

3. Blessed and blessed is that man who opens his mouth to bless and exalt God.

Blasphemous is that man who in the presence of the Lord, every day of his life, opens his mouth to curse and abuse.

5. Blessed and blessed is he who blesses all the works of the Lord.

6. sinner and blasphemer are the ones who despise the mighty creation of God.

7. Blessed and blesses is he who looks down and helps the fallen.

8. Blasphemous and sinful is that man who looks carefully for the destruction of what is not his.

9. Blessed and blessed is he who keeps the principles of his fathers and affirms them from the beginning.

10. Blasphemous and sinful is the one who twists and perverts the mandates of his ancestors.

11. Blessed and blessed is he who sows peace and love.

12. A sinner is a man who upsets those who love their neighbors.

13. Blessed is he who speaks with words and a humble heart.

14. Sinner and blasphemer are he who speaks peace with his mouth, while in his heart there is no peace, but a sword and violence.

15. Well, all these things will be put in evidence, with nothing hidden, in the pan of the balance and the Books, on the day of the great judgment.

1. My children, do not say now: "Our father is praying for our sins because he is before the presence of the Lord" because no helper for any man who is guilty is valid there.

2. Rather, you must observe, how I have written all the actions of every human being, before his creation, all the things that have been done by every human being in all his time, and no one can say or relate what I have written because the Lord looks at all the thoughts that are in the mind of man, as they are in the treasure-houses of each heart.

3. My children, now you must keep and record very well all the words of your father, which I tell you. And you must do it so that you won't lament later saying: "why didn't our father tell us?"

Chapter 54: The Written Books will bring peace.

1. Sadly, in previous times, you did not understand that these books that I have given you should be delivered since these are for an inheritance of your peace that is why he told them:

2. You must pass them on to all the people who yearn for them, and you must also instruct them so that they too can read of the very great and wonderful works of the Lord Almighty.

Chapter 55: It's time for Enoch's departure.

1. Observe, my children, the determined day of my deadline, and the time has come.

2. Now, the angels of the Lord who will travel with me are standing before me, and they urge me to leave, waiting they are standing to be able to fulfill at that was entrusted to them.

3. Because tomorrow, I will ascend to heaven, to the place where the highest Jerusalem is, to my eternal inheritance.

4. It is for all that I beg you with the request, do all the great complacencies before the presence of the Lord.

Chapter 56: Unearthly Food.

1. At that moment, Methuselah answers by asking his father Enoch: What can be done pleasing in your eyes,

father, that I can Carry out before you, so that you can bless our families and houses, and your children, and that you people become glorious through you, and that you can leave like this, as the Lord established?

2. Then Enoch spoke to his son Methuselah saying: "Listen, my son, since the time that the Lord made me anoint myself with the ointment of his glory, I have had no food in me, and therefore my soul has not. Has the memory of earthly enjoyments, neither do I desire anything earthly"?

Chapter 57: Enoch's blessing for his children

1. Now, Methuselah, my son, call and gather all your brothers, and also all your family, the elders of the town, so that I can speak to them and leave, as the Lord as designed for me.

2. So Methuselah ran diligently and called his brothers, Regin, Reman, Uchan, Chermion, Gaidad, and also all the elders of the people before their father Enoch; and it was then that he blessed them, and spoke to them saying:

1. On this day, listen to me, my children.

2. At that time when the Lord descended to earth for the sake of Adam, and visited all his creatures on earth, created by Himself, after this he created Adam. And the Lord called all the animals of the earth, all the reptiles, and all the birds that populated the airs and summoned them before the presence of Adam, our father.

3. And so, Adam named every living thing that inhabited the earth.

4. Also the Lord delegated to him to administer over All Things, these should be subject to his hands, and he made them dumb and slow so that they could be governed by man and be in obedience and subject to his approval.

5. In this way, the Lord created every human being above all his possessions.

6. The Lord taught, that he will not enter into judgment against any soul of the beast because of man, however, he awarded the souls of men to their beasts in this world; because man has a special place.

7. And since each soul of the human being is according to number, similarly, the beasts do not perish, nor any soul of the beast that the Lord created, this will be until the

great judgment, and they can accuse the human being if he hurts them or mistreats.

Chapter 59: Justice with animals

1. Who wants to ham or stain the soul of the beasts, is staining his soul.

2. However, the human being presents clean animals to perform the sacrifices for their sins, so that these can heal their souls.

3. And it happens that when the man brings for sacrifice clean animals and birds, which the man has healed, he heals his soul.

4. Keep in mind that everything is given to you for food, tied by the four legs, that is, to make the cure good, he heals your soul.

5. Worse, everyone who wants to kill animals without any injury, kills his soul, and stains his soul.

6. And anyone who causes any animal any injury anywhere, secretly, this is an unhealthy practice, and he is staining his soul.

1. Anyone who works the death of the soul of a human being has worked the death of his soul and also kills his own body, and there is no solution for him forever.

2. That person who puts another in a problem should first get himself into it, and there is no remedy for that person forever.

3. That human being who puts a man in any matter, his just punishment would not be removed on the day of great justice forever.

4. That person who evilly works or speaks to harm a soul, will not have justice for himself, forever

Chapter 61: Value of integrity in offerings.

1. Listen to me, my children, for you must turn hearts away from all works of injustice that the Lord hates. In the same way that the human being asks God for something for his soul, so let Him do it for every living soul because I know All Things.

As in the great hour that is to come, there are many mansions prepared for the human beings, it will be good for the good, and it will be bad for the bad, and many without number.

2. Blessed and blessed are all those who enter into good things because in bad things there is no peace or return from them.

3. My children, listen to me, all small and all great, children and adults, when the human being puts in his heart a good reason, bringing gifts of his works before the Lord, and his hands do not do good work, then the Lord gives the back to the offering that hose hands present; and in this way, the human being will not be able to find the good work of his hands.

4. Then, his hands do it, inside his heart he murmurs, and his heart does not stop murmuring, then he, does not reach any advantage. That is why the hands and the heart must agree to do well.

Chapter 62: Be careful with vows lightly.

1. Blessed and blessed is that man who with his faith and perseverance presents his offering before the presence of

the Lord because in this way he finds forgiveness for his mistakes.

2. However, if he retracts what he has said ahead of time, there is no longer any regret for his life; and if time passes and he does not go back on what is promised, there will be no chance of repentance after his death.

3. Because all the actions that man performs before the time, are deception before men and guilt before the presence of the Lord.

Chapter 63: The differences between the just and the proud.

1. Good deeds are blessed by the Lord. When someone clothes the one who has no clothes and gives food to the hungry, he finds a reward form God.

2. But if, on the contrary, there is evil in his heart, and he murmurs, he does double harm; he sows ruin for himself and for what he gives, and for him, there will be no reward.

3. And if he only seeks that his heart is full of food and fat, and his own body clothed in good clothes, he commits an outrage, and he will lose all his resistance to poverty, and he will not get a reward for his good deeds.

4. Every person who is proud and arrogant in his words is ungrateful to God. Everyone is false in his speech, and dresses in a suit of deception; he will be cut with the blade of the sword of death; it will be thrown into the fire, and it will be consumed forever.

Chapter 64: Enoch, the man scribe, Redeemer, and Help.

1. Then, when Enoch has finished speaking all these words to his sons, all the people from afar and those from near heard how the Lord was calling Enoch. They took counsel with each other:

2. And they said: "Let's go and kiss Enoch", then at that moment two thousand men united, came to the place called: Achuzan, the place where Enoch and his sons were.

3. Likewise, the elders of his people, the whole assembly, came and bowed and began to kiss Enoch, and spoke to him saying:

4. Our father, Enoch, blessed be you of the Eternal Lord, Almighty, and Governing, bless now your children, and all the people, so that we may be glorified today in your presence

5. because, the truth is that we have understood that you will be glorified before the presence of the Lord, forever, in view that he chose you before any other human being on this earth, and appointed you scribe of all his creation, visible and invisible, and as that redeemer of the sins of the human being and as a help to your immense family.

Chapter 65: The power and beauty of the Great Harmony.

1. At that moment, Enoch opened his mouth responding to all his people: "My children, listen to me before all creatures were created, the Lord created with his power All Things, visible and invisible."

2. And as time went to and on, after all that, he created man in the image of his from and gave him eyes to see, ears to hear, a heart to meditate, and an intellect with which to deliberate, reason and judge.

3. Then, the Lord contemplated all the works, the human being, created all his creatures, also divided the times, of time he fixed the years, of the years he ordered the months, and of the months he assigned the days, and of the days the Lord appointed seven.

4. And in those days the Lord established the hours, took exact measurements of them, so that the human being, the one who had created, could reflect on time and count the years, month, hours, their alterations, beginning and end. End, and also for the purpose that he might recount his very life from its beginning to the time of his death, meditate on his guilt, and write down his good and bad deeds; because no work is hidden before the eyes of the Lord, so that every human being can know his works and never break his commandments and keep my writings from one generation to another generation.

5. And when the time comes, when all creation, visible and invisible, as God established it, comes to an end, then every man will stand before the great tribunal, and by then time will have perished, and the years, and from that moment on there will be neither months, nor days, nor hours, they will join each other, and their account will no longer exist.

6. At that moment, a beautiful harmony will begin, and also all the upright who have fled from the great judgment for the Lord will be gathered in that great harmony, because for the upright the great harmony will begin, and they will live forever, and then there will be no among them work, neither illness, nor humiliation, nor anxiety, nor need, nor violence, nor day, nor any darkness, but there will be a great and resplendent light.

7. They will also have a very large wall and also indestructible, there will also be a paradise full of light and incorruptible, because everything corruptible, all corruptible things will cease to be forever, and everything will come to be eternal life.

Chapter 66: Scripture is to be read and understood.

1. Listen to me carefully, my children, keep your souls out of every act of injustice, the one that displeases the Lord.

2. You must walk before the presence of the Lord, respectful and trembling, and serve only the Lord.

3. You must give honor and reverence to the true God, not to the vain and foolish idols, respect the image of the image of God and bring only offerings before the Lord. God rejects and abhors all injustice.

4. Always keep in mind, that the Lord observes and knows all things when he receives the thoughts in his heart, then be directs the intellects and every thought is always before him, the One who firmly established the earth, and placed all its creatures about her.

5. Keep the truth in your heart, if you look to heaven, the Lord is there; and if you become aware of the depth of

the ocean and everything that is under the earth, keep in mind that the Lord is there.

6. Well, the Eternal and Almighty Lord is the creator of All Things, Therefore, you should not give honor and reverence to things made by human hands, thereby leaving the Lord of all creation, because no work can remain hidden before the presence of the Lord.

7. With attention, listen to me my children, you must walk in humility and meekness, in faith and honesty, in truth, in security over promises, in illness, in abuse, in wounds, in temptation, in nakedness, in privation, giving love to the other until you get out of this age of evils, so that you become heirs of that time without end, eternal

8. Blessed and blessed are righteous who escape the great judgment, because they will be the ones who will shine much more than the sevenfold of the Sun, because in this world the seventh part is taken from the whole, light, darkness, food, rejoicing, sadness, paradise, torture, fire, frost, among other things, he put everything in writing so that you could read and understand All Things.

Chapter 67; Enoch is raised to the Highest Heaven. The Unseen God.

1. And after Enoch had spoken with his people, the Lord sent darkness over the earth, and that darkness enveloped all those people who accompanied and were piped with Enoch, those men took Enoch and took him to the highest of the heaven, where is the abode of the Lord.

And he received it and set it before him, then the darkness disappeared from the earth, and again the light shone.

2. And all those people could see it, but they could not understand how Enoch had been taken, so they glorified God, and found a written record where it was written "The invisible God", and in this way, they all returned to their homes.

Chapter 68: sign of Enoch for the last generation and those to come.

1. Enoch was raised to heaven on the first day the month Tesivan, and he was in heaven for sixty days.

2. Enoch recorded in this writings what corresponds to all the signs of all creation, which the Eternal Lord created, and wrote three hundred and sixty-six books, and gave them to his children and was on earth thirty days, and he

was again raised to heaven on the sixth day of the month Tesivan on the same day and hour in which he was born.

3. Just as the nature of every human being in this life is dark, so are their arguments, their birth, and their departure from this earth

4. And in the hour that he was conceived, in that same hour, he expired

5. So Methuselah and all his brothers, all the sons of Enoch, diligently hastened and erected an altar in the place called Achuzan, whence Enoch was raised to the heights of heaven.

6. So they took oxen to sacrifice, and called all the people, and presented the sacrifice as an offering before the presence of the Lord.

7. All the people, all the elders of Enoch's people, and the whole assembly came to the banquet and brought gifts to Enoch's sons.

8. and they made great party for three days, all rejoiced with great joy, and praised the Lord who had sent them this sign through Enoch, a man who found favor with El, a sign that they should pass on to their children, from generation to generation, from age to age for all time.

The Bible itself as a book that keeps ancient records and refers to the most remote times teaches us that there were giants on earth before the flood, and also after that judgment, let's see:

Genesis 6:4 "There were giants on the earth in those days, and also after sons of God came to the daughters of men, and bore children to them. "Later, the Bible mentions other giants in the land of Canaan, and in the time of King David.

Within the apocryphal literature, the book of Baruch 3:24-27 tells us: "O Israel, how great is the house of God, and how vast is his domain. It is very big and has no end. Giants were born there, famous since ancient times, tall, and skilled in war. But, God did not choose these, nor did he make known to them the way of wisdom, and thus they perished for lack of prudence.

Without a doubt, these giants generated a lot of fear, to the point, among the Israelites of not want to fight against them. Other peoples also knew and feared these giants, whom they called: Enaquitas, Refaitas, and Emitas, among others.

Other texts of the Bible and many ancient records allow us to see their lifestyle, that is, they lived in cities (sometimes large), raised families, and worked with stone and metals. They were also very good warriors, some famous giants were:

Og, King of Bashan.
Arbé was famous among his people
Goliath and Dodo, are strong and famous warrior who militated in the ranks of the Philistine army.
Rafa, ancestor, and patriarch of other men of great stature.
The disappearance of these giants is still very interesting for silence.

Archaeological finds:

The discovery of large human skeletons or remains seems to confirm that in ancient time's areas of the earth were inhabited by giants; and of course, many traditions and cultures tell stories that narrate the presence and exploits of these giants.

We find historical records of these beings in the bible, in sacred texts from Thailand, in Greek mythology, in the Aztec, Egyptian, and European cultures, etc. its palpable footprint through the remains of its immense and ancient constructions.

Through remains found throughout the North American territory, this truth is palpable. For example, in the year 1883, some soldiers removed in the state of Nevada, the remains of a man of three and a half meters. In 1993, the petrified remains of two giants 4.5 and 5.5 meters high were unearthed in Arizona (in the Grand Canyon).

Giant remains have been found in Central and South America. For example in the Gold Museum of Lima Peru, a gigantic human skull is preserved.

 Other remains and finds can be seen in the UK and in Ireland. In Chenini Tunisia, a graveyard of three-meter giants was discovered.

In the city of Bathurst (Australia) a gigantic molar was found, along with some tools, which, according to experts, could have belonged to a human being 7.5 meters tall and about five hundred kilograms in weight.

The five giants that stood out in the Bible:

It is very important to keep in mind that when Israel began the conquest of the Promised Land, one of the things that discouraged the Hebrew people is that the ten spies spoke of the giants that lived there, and that said they were so big and powerful that they could not they could beat them.

Who was Goliath, the Philistine giant?

This giant was a leading soldier in the Philistine army. His name "Goliath" and the root of this word, allows us to see several meanings:
The one who takes captives and spoils them
Banishment (who he takes captive)
Rebellion (does not submit to God and promotes disobedience)

Goliath was a Philistine, and the Philistine were a warrior nation, so there was often war between the Philistine and the Israelites. The Philistine were idolaters, their main gods were Dagon, Ashtoreth, and Beelzebub; Dagon being the most important to them. Goliath himself was a worshiper of those gods, 1 Samuel 17:42-43 tell us.

"And when the Philistine looked and saw David, he thought little of him; because he was a boy, and blond, and handsome in appearance. And the Philistine said to David: Am I a dog that you come to me with sticks? And he cursed David by his gods."

The giant Sipai:

1 Chronicle 20:4 tells us "After this, was broke out in Gezer against the Philistines; and Sibecai Husatite killed Sipai of the descendants of the giants, and they were humiliated."

The battle takes place in Gezer. The word "Gezer" means portion, something cut, or separated. The city that was for centuries in Canaanite hand, and was assigned to the Levites, who for a long time could not use it. It was given by God to the Levites, but the descendants of the giants did not want to give it up. The giant Sipai was there to prevent the priestly functions of the Levites.

That giant is called Sipai. This name means Guard of the threshold or the main door. Bowl of vessel that contains. Sipai prevents access or controls passage.
He is defeated by Sibeki a Hushatite. The root of the name "Sibecai" means: wrap, interweave. In the Bible, it is used in two verses to refer to the interweaving (braiding) that forms the branches or roots of a tree.

The interwoven branches provide shade and cushion a fall, the interwoven or braided roots are stronger to support a large tree and are extremely difficult to uproot. This tells us about the importance of unity, of love towards the brother, of the ability to forgive the other.

The giant Lahmi brother of Goliath:

1 Chronicles 20:5 tells us "Again war broke out against the Philistines; and Elhanan son of Jair killed Lahmi, brother of Goliath the Gitite, whose spear shaft was like a loom roller".

The giant Lahmi had a great spear just like his brother's with which he wanted to instill fear, but Elhanan went to fight with faith, as David did, and thus triumphed.

Lahmi, the Philistine giant, was the brother of Goliath the Getite (name of the inhabitant of Gat, as 1 Samuel 17:4 "Goliath of Gath" tell us), a giant who fell defeated by the hand of David. Perhaps he acted in this giant, a spirit of revenge.

Second, let's see the meaning of his name. His name "Lahmi" has several meanings: My bread (the root of the word translates: food). My was Warrior. It is one that hinders food for God's people.

Elhanán, the warrior who defeated him, has several meanings: Grace. God has shown his favor. Gift "son of Jair" and the name Jair means: "My light" "Who spreads light" "Illuminated by God".

The giant with six fingers on his hand and feet:

1 Chronicles 20:6 tells us "And there was war again in Gath, where there was a man of great stature, who had six fingers and toes, twenty-four in all; and he was a descendant of the giants".

The city of Gat was under the Philistine rule, for certain periods of time it was under the government of Israel. Its name "Gat" means Grape press, press or wine vat. That was fertile land and there were many vineyards and grape presses. It is significant that Goliath was from there, as well as this giant.

In the Bible, the name of this giant is not given, unlike the previous ones, such as Goliath, Sipai, and Lahmi, The fact that his name is unknown allows us to conclude that he works covertly, he does not reveal his true purposes, but rather he works in a hidden way.

It is very interesting to note that it had six fingers on each of its limbs, for a total of "twenty-four fingers for all" as the Bible tells us.

In Scripture the number six refers to the human, it is the imperfect number (because the perfect number is 7); it is humanism that displaces God; 666 is the number of the antichrist, so the reference is made here to one or that which is not aligned with God, is not in accordance with the design of the Lord, is opposed to God.

1 Chronicles 30:7 "This man reviled Israel, but Jonathan son of Shimea, David's brother, killed him".

This giant fell before Jonathan son of Shimea. His name "Jonathan" means: God has given. God has established; and Simea means proclamation, testimony, and word. By uniting these meanings we can summarize what Jonathan son of Simea means: that God has given his testimony, God has established his word, and it was before this man that the giant fell.

The giant Isbi-benob.

Philistine enemies. 2 Samuel 21:15

"Moreover the Philistine had yet war again with Israel, and David went down, and his servants with him, and fought against the Philistines: and David waxed faint".

First of all, we must take into account that the Philistine people were inhabitants of before the Hebrews in Canaanite lands. His main activity was fishing, so his god Dagon was half man and half fish. A people of pagan customs, and an enemy of the Hebrew people.

The word "philistine" shows their love for their gods: Dagon, Beelzebub, and Astarte. Inhabitants of the shore of the Mediterranean Sea, historically known as Phoenicia. His military success was due to the secret knowledge and monopoly of the iron foundry (weapons, tools, etc).

Their cities were: Gaza, Ashdod, Ashkelon, Ekron, and Gath. Let us remember that this last city, Gat, was the Philistine giant that David initially defeated, that is why the Bible presents him as Goliath of Gath. Also, Delilah was a Philistine.

Etymologically, the word "philistine" comes from the Hebrew "pilistim" and the Greek "Philistenoi", precedents of the term "Palestinian", opponents of the Hebrew people today.

Considering what 2 Samuel 21:15 tells us, the enemy Philistine people periodically attacked Israel, and this was one more occasion. David reigned and comes with his soldiers and officers to face the enemy.

We must highlight a very important phrase in this verse: "and David grew weary" The battles demand a lot of effort from the soldiers until they are exhausted; King David got tired, and his strength diminished significantly, and this undoubtedly made his more vulnerable.

The Bible warns us that we cannot ignore the plans of the enemy; the kingdom of darkness seeks through many strategies to exhaust the son of God, which makes him less effective in his service to the Lord, strength to advance and makes him weak and vulnerable to his attacks.

That is why our communion with God is so important because there, we are renewed, strengthened, and anointed to advance and overcome all opposition and all the obstacles of the path of faith.

Beware of Isbi-benob, 2 Samuel 21-16

"And Ishbibenob, which was of the sons of the giant, the weight of whose spear weighed three hundred shekels of brass in weight, he being girded with a new sword, thought to have slain David".

The Scripture now tells us that a descendant of the giants tried to kill David. It is interesting that he did not come at the beginning of the battle, but when David was tired. So exhausting the son of God a battle strategy before attempting his true destruction.

We must also keep in mind that he was a descendant of the Philistine giants, and I believe, that he was also motivated by a spirit of revenge, perhaps he wanted to get even with David for the death of Goliath.

Sometimes the enemy plants seeds of hatred in other people against us, to which we must respond with a spiritual perspective since we do not fight against flesh and blood, but against unclean spirits.

We can see this giant as the enemy that exhausts and wears down the Christian before attacking him with force. His name Isbi-benob also means the one who takes captive. An exhausted person is easy to take captive or prisoner
With a spear and a new sword, he tried to kill David.

It is very interesting that the Hebrew word that is translated here as "tried" is "to love", a word that also means: to speak, to say, to order. Well, it is meaning that allows us to think of at least two things:

First, this giant did not act alone but spoke with others to exhaust and wear David down before attacking him, since he knew that Goliath had died at David's hand.

And second, speaking and saying are actions in which we express words that carry a message. Let us remember that the Bible warns us about the fiery darts of the evil one, which are words and messages from the devil that come against the mind to attack our faith in Christ Jesus.

 If you add doubt and uncertainty to exhaustion, you will have a tired and fearful soldier, without strength and afraid to advance and fight. A soldier who will easily flee at the first battle cry.

Isbi-benob come with every intention of killing the King of Israel. David is a name that means beloved. Represents praise, David is an ancestor of Jesus, from his offspring our Savior would come, Jesus Christ the Lord.

In a spiritual sense, we can say that this giant seeks to destroy praise and love for God, and also seeks to destroy the seed or offspring of God. Our children are offspring of the Lord's plans on this earth, and for this reason, we must instruct them in the fear of God and cover them in prayer.

The fall of the giant. 2 Samuel 21:17

"But Abishai the son of Zeruiah succored him, and smote the Philistine, and killed him. Then the men of David swore unto him, saying, Thou shalt go no more out with us to battle, that thou quench not the light of Israel".

This verse reminds us that God never forsakes us, his powerful hand preserves us according to his plans and purposes. David was about to die at the hands of this giant, but this was not David's time to go the presence of God.

The word of the Lord tells us that just at that moment, Abishai, son of Sarvia, came to help David; who wounded the giant and killed him. The name "Abishai" means: My father God exists. It reminds us of this, that our Father God never forsakes of abandons us.

Abishai represents the hand of God that helps us in a moment of mortal crisis, those moments in which we find ourselves incapable and without strength, exhausted, and without solutions. It is God's help that arrives, not only at the right time but with all the power to bring down the giant that rises up and wants to stop us.

We speaks of that giant who wants to usurp what God has given us, who wants to take the blessing that the Lord has given us, and who tries to prevent us from enjoying the inheritance that we have in Christ.

We must keep in mind that the Philistines were neighbors of Israel, and they came to make war against the Hebrews to make them go back and strip them of the land that God had promised them, the land of blessing, land that flows with milk and honey.

But, God had given a word to his people: "I gave them the land flowing with milk and honey", and there is no enemy, no giant, no power on this earth, nor in the entire universe that can stop the will of God, and everything he has said will be fulfilled, and every giant will fall and every obstacle will disappear, because he is with us. Jehovah of hosts.

At the end of verse 17, we are told that David's soldiers said to him, "you are the light of the world". The lamps of that time could not work without oil, the fire needs oil, it is interesting that both fire and oil in the Bible are symbols of the Holy Spirit. No wonder Paul said, "Rather be filled with the Spirit".

We need to be enlivened by the fire of the Holy Spirit, to be anointed with the oil of the Spirit of God; therefore, the Lord sent his Spirit into our lives.

God has not given us a spirit of cowardice but of power, love, and dominion, our own; through him and in Christ we can advance and win, and if any giant has risen in your life, remember, he was a son of God and the heavenly Father is on your side, and the enemy will fall in the name of Jesus.

We must finally keep in mind that the Lord Jesus has given us authority over our enemies, and in his name, we can overcome any giant that rises up against us and wants to stop our advance:

Luke 10:19 "Behold, I give you the power to tread on serpents and scorpions, and over all the power of the enemy, and nothing will harm you".

Let us note that his passage tells us: "and over all the strength of the enemy", understanding the enemy as anyone or anything that opposes and rises up against the purposes of God for our lives.

Conclusion: we cannot ignore the plans and machinations of the enemy; thanks God, we have been equipped to overcome every obstacle, and bring down every giant in the name of the Lord Jesus Christ. Advance, trust in God, he has prepared powerful victories and great conquests for you.

In the diversity of peoples, cultures, and religious beliefs, we find multiple concepts of an evil being or several of them, in Judaism, the devil is known as a fallen angel or demon, and in other cultures, and he has considered a god of evil expelled from heaven.

The origin of Satan according to the Holy Scriptures:

The first thing we must consider is the meaning of the word "Satan", from the original Hebrew biblical term (and even from the Greek) translated: opponent, enemy, adversary, and accuser (the root of the Hebrew word means: attack, accuse, slander).

Meanwhile, the term "devil" in Biblical Greek is "diabolos" and translated slanderer, loves of malicious gossip, the false accuser (the root of the word indicates one who attacks by spewing slander, causing another to be accused or condemned).

The names with which it is indicated in the Bible are diverse for example: "And he seized the dragon, the old serpent, who is the devil and Satan, and bound him for a thousand years", Revelation 20:2.

Regarding the origin of Satan, we can say that he was initially a beautiful creation of God, like an anointed cherub, resplendent, and with great privileges in heaven.

The prophet Ezekiel declares this prophecy at the beginning for the king of Tyre, but soon the prophet leads us by Spirit to see the fall of the cherub who one day rebelled and became the devil and Satan:

"The word of the Lord came to me, saying, Son of man, lift dirges against the king of Tyre, and say to him, thus says the Lord God: You were the seal of perfection, full of wisdom, and finished in beauty. In Eden, in the garden of God, you were; your clothing was made of every precious stone... emerald and gold; the beauties of your drums and flutes were prepared for you on the day of your creation" Ezekiel 28:11-13.

Since the beginning of the Christian church, this passage has been interpreted as an allusion to the fall of Satan.

In the text of the Bible, Ezekiel 28:11-19, we can highlight several very important aspects:

This cherub was created in a state of perfection, verse twelve declares: "seal of perfection", an expression that also means: exemplary seal, model to follow, blueprint.

He was in Eden, according to verse thirteen. Her dress was built in gold and with nine precious stones. These are nine of the twelve that were on the garment of the Levitical high priest, as well as the gold.

Some biblical versions translate the last part as other accessories that were prepared for the day of its creation (earrings, pendants, settings, jewelry, carved ornaments), and do not translate these terms as musical instruments, that is, not as "flutes and drums").

As the Bible tells us, he was a cherub, with a high level of authority and privilege, as the verse of Ezekiel 28:14 tells us "You, great cherub, protector, I put you on the Holy mountain of God, there you were; amid the stones of fire, you walked.

He was a cherub of integrity from the day of his creation until he fell into wickedness, iniquity, or injustice (we do not know how long this took). Ezekiel 18:15 "You were perfect in all your ways from the day you were created, until iniquity was found in you".

Verse sixteen lets us see a little more about the reasons or factors of his fall when he tells us "Because of the multitude of your hiring's you were full of iniquity, and you sinned, because of what I threw you out of the mountain of God", the version of the Bible of the Americas translated here: "abundance of your commerce".

Verse seventeen of Ezekiel twenty-eight teaches us that the heart of this cherub was lifted, that is, he was filled with pride, haughtiness and had ambitious plans, desiring the very throne of his Creator:

"Your heart was lifted because of your beauty, you corrupted your wisdom because of your splendor; I will throw you to the ground, I will place you before kings so that they may look at you." Ezekiel 28:16.

Let us now consider the fall of Satan from Isaiah 14:12-15

"How did you fall from heaven, oh Lucero, son of the morning? You were cut down to the ground, you who weakened the nations. You who said in your heart: I will ascend to heaven; on high, by the stars of God, I will raise my throne, and I will sit, on the sides of the north; I will ascend above the heights of the clouds, and I will be like the Most High. But you are cast down to Seol, to the sides of the abyss".

The prophet Isaiah initially declares this word for the king of Babylon, but then reveals truths far beyond. The Christian church also sees here a revelation of the Spirit about the fall of Satan.

The biblical text describes the initial name of: "Lucero", and ads "son of the morning" or "son of the dawn". The Hebrew term "Lucero" means: bright, resplendent (the Version of the Bible of the Americas has the expression: "the shining").

In the Book of the prophet Isaiah fourteen, verses thirteen and fourteen allow us to see his ambition and ego: "You who said in your heart: I will ascend to heaven: on high, by the stars of God, I will raise my throne, and on the amount of testimony I will sit, on the sides of the north; I will ascend above the heights of the clouds, and I will be like the Most High".

It is interesting to note that the biblical passage reveals Satan's intentions and motives, which is why he uses the expression "I will be like the Most High" (Isaiah 14:14), and here "Most High" is translated from the Hebrew word "Elion", the word that also means: Supreme, high, superior, the highest.

So, this cherub was not interested in the pastoral work of the Lord, nor his love for his people, nor the care for his children, or anything like that, he wanted to be the highest, the superior, he wanted to be the supreme.

It is precisely this that he uses to get to rule the human heart because in general, the human heart wants the first place, most important, each one seeks his own. It is very interesting to remember here the words of Jesus:

"I won't talk much with you anymore; because the prince of this world is coming, and he has nothing in me" John 14:30.

Some expose the beginning of creation "The Gap Theory" between Genesis 1:1 and 1:2.
1 "In the beginning, God created the heavens and the earth.

2 And the earth was without form and void, and darkness was over the face of the deep, and the Spirit of God moved over the face of the waters".

This theory states that between verses on and two of Genesis one, there is a space where Satan's rebellion took place, and God sent a first flood that left the earth disordered and empty.

This is an exposition with a little biblical foundation and without much scriptural basis (and several times inconsistent). It contains gaps and spaces, without a clear and forceful answer.

This thought was proposed in the year 1814 by Thomas Chalmers of the University of Edinburgh in Scotland (it is not an exposition of the early church, Jesus did not mention such a thing, nor was it an apostolic doctrine).

Proponents of the gap theory posit that a cataclysmic judgment was decreed on Earth as a result of the fall of Lucifer (Satan) and that the subsequent verses of Genesis chapter 1 describe a re-ordering of Earth from a state chaotic. Some call this the luciferian flood.

Its main basis in the terms with which the state of the earth in Genesis 1:2 is described as "formless and empty" (the biblical Hebrew words used here are: "tohu and bohu"), they say that God did not create it thus, according to Isaiah 45:18, where we are told:

"for thus saith the Lord, who create the heavens; he is God, the one who formed the earth, the one who made it and composed it; he did not create it in vain, he created it to be inhabited: I am the Lord, and there is no other."

So, they teach that Lucero ruled the earth, over a generation of beings that inhabited it. By rebelling against God he was expelled from Eden and became a devil and Satan, and his followers became demons.

God sent his judgment on the earth through a fist flood (Noah's would be the second), and that is why the biblical text says that the earth was covered with water. The textual composition does not entirely favor this theory.

This position is not strongly held in the Scriptures. Nor has it been a doctrine of the first Christian church, nor current.

The Lord Jesus himself taught that the lake of fire was designed for the devil and those angles who rebelled: "Then he will also say to those on the left: Depart from me, you cursed, into the eternal fire prepared for the devil and his angles" Matthew 25:41.

The Bible tells us about prisons of darkness and prisons In Hades, regarding infernal prisons, we can see the following characteristics:

Meaning of some terms
Sheol: Hebrew term for the place where all the dead went.
Hades: Greek term to refer to the same place.

Hell: the term used to refer to the place of torment for those who do not avail themselves of the grace of God in Christ. It is synonymous with Hades.

Prisons of darkness:

Where the fallen angels of 2 Peter 2:4, are confined for the final judgment (otherwise they would continue taking earthly women, contaminating and altering the seed of God, promoting a large-scale human perversion of these times, and seeking its destruction, as they did in the flood).

In biblical Greek the word used is "tartaroo", some versions translate: dungeons, it is the deepest place in Hades.

Abyss:

Translates from the Greek word "abusso", which refers to an unfathomable depth, the lower world, the infernal regions, and the abyss of Sheol (deep well)

Revelation 20:1-3 teaches us that it is a spiritual prison where the devil is imprisoned for a thousand years, "I saw an angel descending from heaven, having the key to the abyss and a great chain in his hand. Ann he seized the dragon, the old serpent, who is the devil and Satan, and bound him for a thousand years; and he cast him into the abyss, and shut him up, and set his seal on him, that he should deceive the nations no more..."

The abyss is then a section of Sheol, as a Tartarus. The demons are afraid to go to this place: Luke 8:30-31 "... Many demons had entered it. And they begged him to send them to the abyss".

This section contains the locusts that will torment men in the great tribulation: Revelation 9:1-6, 11 and their king is the angel of the abyss, called Abaddon and Apollyon in Greek (terms that mean: destroyer).

Lake of fire:

This expression indicates the place of final and eternal punishment for the devil, his angels, and all the wicked, Revelation 20:11-15

"And death and Hades were cast into the lake of fire. This is the second death. And whoever was not found written in the book of life was cast into the lake of fire". Revelation 20:14-15.